Grow your English skills with CGP

Pupils have to dig deep to master all the English skills they need for Year 2 — which means lots of practice. Handily, this CGP book is overflowing with it.

From poems to present tense, it's loaded with activities that test topics from the Year 2 curriculum. With one page for every day of the spring term, it's a practice powerhouse!

'Ding ding ding!' — bonus alert! It's also got bright pictures, engaging comprehension texts and handy examples. Use it in class, at home, on a boat, in a hot air balloon...

What CGP is all about

Our sole aim here at CGP is to produce the highest quality books
— carefully written, immaculately presented and
dangerously close to being funny.

Then we work our socks off to get them out to you
— at the cheapest possible prices.

Contents

☑ Use the tick boxes to help keep a record of which tests have been attempted.

Week 1
- ☑ Day 1 1
- ☑ Day 2 2
- ☑ Day 3 3
- ☑ Day 4 4
- ☑ Day 5 5

Week 2
- ☑ Day 1 6
- ☑ Day 2 7
- ☑ Day 3 8
- ☑ Day 4 9
- ☑ Day 5 10

Week 3
- ☑ Day 1 11
- ☑ Day 2 12
- ☑ Day 3 13
- ☑ Day 4 14
- ☑ Day 5 15

Week 4
- ☑ Day 1 16
- ☑ Day 2 17
- ☑ Day 3 18
- ☑ Day 4 19
- ☑ Day 5 20

Week 5
- ☑ Day 1 21
- ☑ Day 2 22
- ☑ Day 3 23
- ☑ Day 4 24
- ☑ Day 5 25

Week 6
- ☑ Day 1 26
- ☑ Day 2 27
- ☑ Day 3 28
- ☑ Day 4 29
- ☑ Day 5 30

Week 7
- ☑ Day 1 31
- ☑ Day 2 32
- ☑ Day 3 33
- ☑ Day 4 34
- ☑ Day 5 35

Week 8
- ☑ Day 1 36
- ☑ Day 2 37
- ☑ Day 3 38
- ☑ Day 4 39
- ☑ Day 5 40

Week 9
- ☑ Day 1 41
- ☑ Day 2 42
- ☑ Day 3 43
- ☑ Day 4 44
- ☑ Day 5 45

Week 10
- ☑ Day 1 46
- ☑ Day 2 47
- ☑ Day 3 48
- ☑ Day 4 49
- ☑ Day 5 50

Week 11
- ☑ Day 1 51
- ☑ Day 2 52
- ☑ Day 3 53
- ☑ Day 4 54
- ☑ Day 5 55

Week 12
- ☑ Day 1 56
- ☑ Day 2 57
- ☑ Day 3 58
- ☑ Day 4 59
- ☑ Day 5 60

Answers 61

Published by CGP

ISBN: 978 1 78908 679 9

Editors: Izzy Bowen, Eleanor Claringbold, Rachel Craig-McFeely, Rebecca Russell, Sean Walsh

With thanks to Juliette Green and Holly Robinson for the proofreading.

With thanks to Lottie Edwards for the copyright research.

Cover and Graphics used throughout the book © www.edu-clips.com

Printed by Bell & Bain Ltd, Glasgow.
Based on the classic CGP style created by Richard Parsons.

Text, design, layout and original illustrations © Coordination Group Publications Ltd. (CGP) 2020
All rights reserved.

CGP, Broughton House, Griffin Street, Broughton-in-Furness, Cumbria, LA20 6HH. EU Rep: International Associates Auditing & Certification Limited, The Black Church, St Mary's Place, Dublin 7, D07 P4AX, Ireland. EUAR@ie.ia-net.com

Photocopying this book is not permitted, even if you have a CLA licence.
Extra copies are available from CGP with next day delivery • 0800 1712 712 • www.cgpbooks.co.uk

How to Use this Book

- This book contains 60 pages of daily English practice.

- We've split them into 12 sections — that's roughly one for each week of the Year 2 Spring term.

- Each week is made up of 5 pages, so there's one for every school day of the term (Monday – Friday).

- Each page should take about 10 minutes to complete.

- The pages contain a mix of topics from Year 2 English. New Year 2 topics are gradually introduced as you go through the book.

- The pages increase in difficulty as you progress through the book.

- Answers can be found at the back of the book.

- Each page looks something like this:

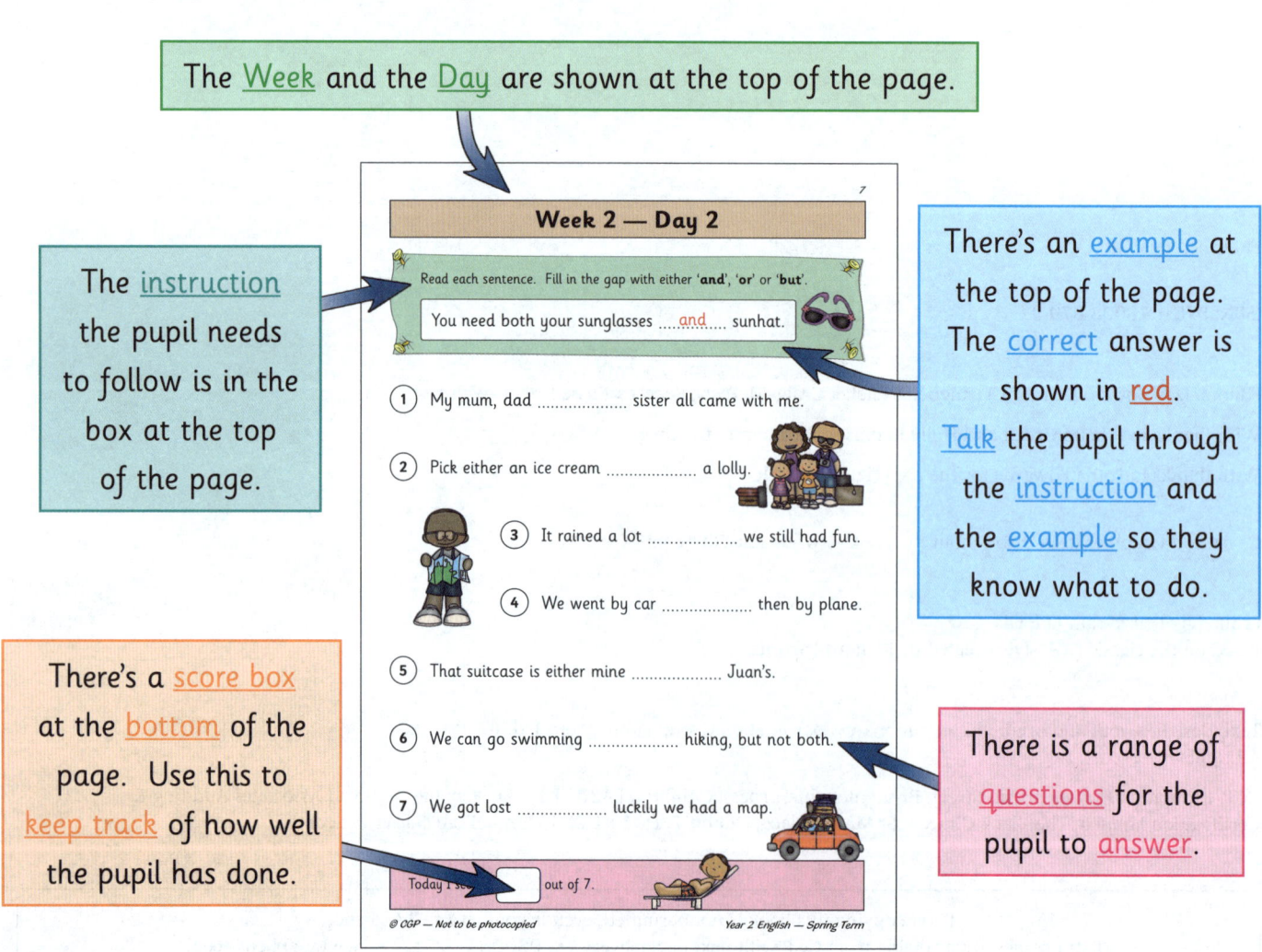

Week 1 — Day 1

Read the sentence. Then circle the letter or letters missing from the word.

I __ocked over a pot. (kn) n

1) There is an interesting **foss**__ here.   il   el

2) Do you __**ow** where the vase is from?   n   kn

3) My brother prefers the **scien**__ museum.   ce   se

4) The **rub**__ are in the museum.   ys   ies

5) The statue is **hu**__.   ge   dge

6) They dug up some old **met**__ tools.   el   al

7) The old __**iting** is interesting.   r   wr

8) There are a lot of **peop**__ here.   al   le

Today I scored ☐ out of 8.

Week 1 — Day 2

Underline the word in each sentence that should have a capital letter.

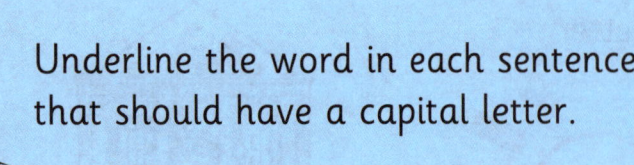

1) maria always wanted to be a ballerina.

2) The best dancer in the class is steve.

3) I do tap dancing every monday.

4) My brother and i love to dance.

5) my tap teacher is a beautiful dancer.

6) Sonya studies dance in russia.

7) I danced with ed.

8) I went to see a dance show in paris.

9) My mum told me the show is on sunday.

10) there is a tiny dancer in the music box.

Today I scored ☐ out of 10.

Week 1 — Day 3

Help each ladybird find the correct leaf by matching the words that fit together to make a longer word. Write your own ending for the final ladybird.

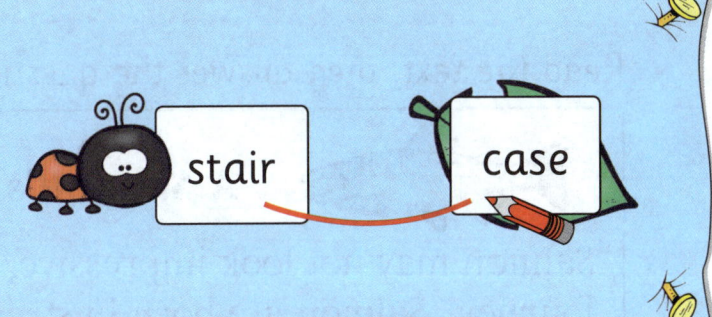

 1 finger

 2 rain

 3 sun

 4 eye

 5 sea

 6 star

 7 butter

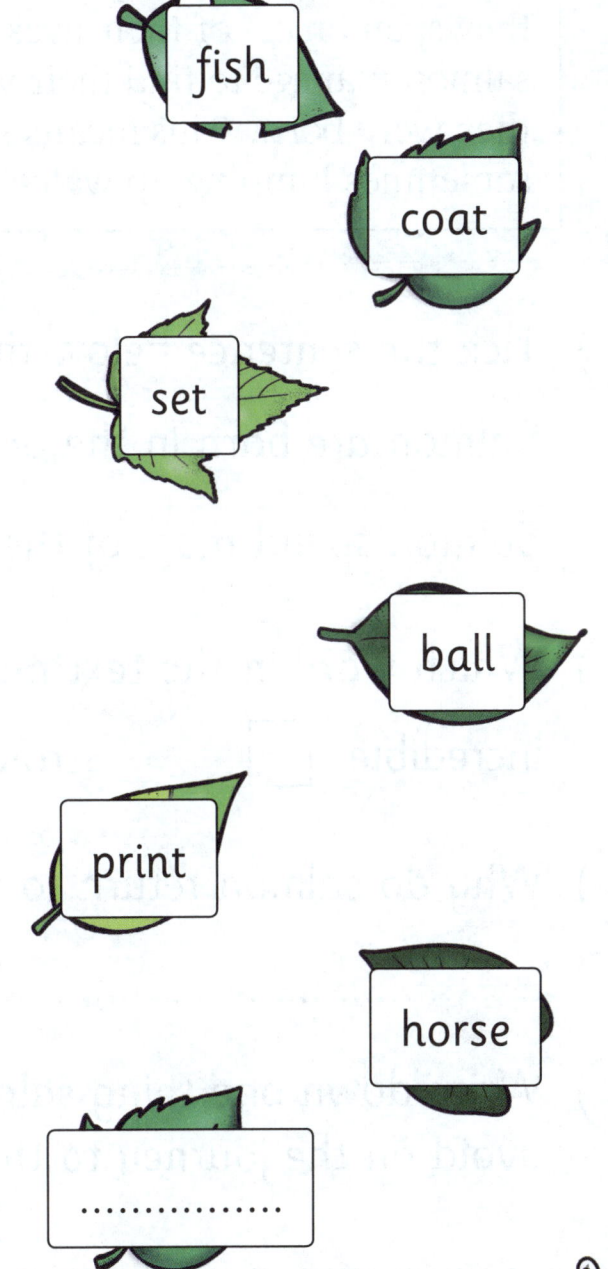

Today I scored ☐ out of 7.

Week 1 — Day 4

Read the text, then answer the questions.

A Salmon's Journey

Salmon may not look impressive, but they make an incredible journey. Salmon are born in streams and rivers, but once they are strong enough, they swim to the ocean. This is where they spend most of their lives. When it's time to lay eggs, salmon manage to find their way back to the exact same spot they were born. This means swimming thousands of miles, sometimes jumping up waterfalls and avoiding hungry bears!

1) Tick the sentence below that is true.

Salmon are born in the ocean. ☐

Salmon spend most of their lives in the ocean. ☐

2) Which word in the text means the same as 'amazing'?

incredible ☐   strong ☐   exact ☐

3) Why do salmon return to their place of birth?

....

4) Write down one thing salmon might have to avoid on the journey to their place of birth.

....

Today I scored ☐ out of 4.

Week 1 — Day 5

Read the text, then answer the questions.

A Sneaky Swan

Percy was a **greedey** swan. He loved living by the lakeside café because he could munch on the crumbs. The grumpy café owner always shooed him away though. One day, Percy was paddling in the lake when he saw a **littal** girl eating an ice cream. He looked around. The café owner was nowhere to be seen. Percy quietly snuck up behind the girl and then... CHOMP! The ice cream was gone.

(1) Give the correct spelling of the words in bold.

greedey .... **littal** ....

(2) What tense is the text written in?

past tense ☐   present tense ☐

(3) Who do you think Percy is looking for when he looks around?

....

(4) What do you think happened to the ice cream?

....

Today I scored ☐ out of 5.

Week 2 — Day 1

Read each sentence. Then circle the correct spelling of the word in bold.

She is the (**writer**) / **riter**.

1) Tom **carried** / **carryed** some books.

2) There are two **librarys** / **libraries** in our town.

3) We read the first **padge** / **page** together.

4) They tried to make the bird **fly** / **flie** away.

5) Anna's books began to **wobbel** / **wobble**.

6) I **placed** / **plased** the book back on the shelf.

7) Yasmin returned the **funy** / **funny** book.

8) She is **smiling** / **smileing** about the story.

9) My book is about a **nome** / **gnome**.

Today I scored ☐ out of 9.

Week 2 — Day 2

Read each sentence. Fill in the gap with either '**and**', '**or**' or '**but**'.

You need both your sunglasses ......*and*...... sunhat.

1) My mum, dad .... sister all came with me.

2) Pick either an ice cream .... a lolly.

3) It rained a lot .... we still had fun.

4) We went by car .... then by plane.

5) That suitcase is either mine .... Juan's.

6) We can go swimming .... hiking, but not both.

7) We got lost .... luckily we had a map.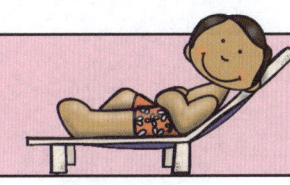

Today I scored ☐ out of 7.

Week 2 — Day 3

Use the words from the boxes to complete the sentences below. You should only use each word once.

smaller   Flutes are ....smaller........ than pianos.

loudest   shinier   harder

easiest   quieter   fastest

1) Eva polished her flute to make it ....

2) Shhh, this part of the music is ....

3) The trumpets made the .... sound.

4) Umar found this part the .... to play.

5) Lea hit the drum .... to make more noise.

6) Hurry, this part should be the ....

Today I scored [ ] out of 6.

Week 2 — Day 4

Read the text, then answer the questions.

Animals at Night

Many animals sleep at night and move around in the day. However, others sleep in the day and move around at night. These include foxes, who sneak around streets looking for food as night falls. You might also see badgers and bats. Small animals like mice and shrews also come out at night. They are hunted by owls who swoop down from the sky. At night time, listen out for an owl's call as it goes 'twit twoo'.

1) According to the text, where might you see a fox at night?

   on streets ☐   in their dens ☐

2) Tick two other animals the text says you can see at night.

   sparrows ☐   bats ☐   mice ☐   bees ☐

3) Based on the text, why do you think owls hunt at night?

   ....

   ....

4) What sound does an owl make?

   ....

Today I scored ☐ out of 5.

Week 2 — Day 5

Read the text, then answer the questions.

The Secret Hideout

Kim liked to hide in secret places. She once built a den with her friend Misha using a tent and some leaves. She also had her own tree house, which was closer to the sky than her actual house.

One day, Kim decided to build her best hideout ever. She used branches to create the frame and then covered it in an old cloth.

"No one will find me here," she whispered.

1) Circle the correct word to complete this sentence.

Kim's treehouse is **higher / lower** than her actual house.

2) Give one thing Kim and Misha used to make their den.

....

3) Which word could be used to join the sentences below?

Kim opened up her book. She started to read it in the quietness of her hideout.

and ☐   or ☐   but ☐

4) Tick the sentence that is true.

Kim isn't sure if she will be found. ☐

Kim thinks that she won't be found. ☐

Today I scored ☐ out of 4.

Week 3 — Day 1

Use the sentences to help you fill in the missing letters in the crossword below.

Flora drinks orange **ju__e**.

| j | u | i | c | e |

1) Please pass the butter **__ife**.

2) Jordan had a **fr___** egg for breakfast.

3) I love **bag__s** with cream cheese.

4) Rami has milk with his **cere__**.

5) There is yoghurt in the **fri___**.

6) Can you boil the **kett__**?

Today I scored [ ] out of 6.

Week 3 — Day 2

The words in bold below are spelt incorrectly.
Write the correct spellings on the lines.

My costume is **fansy**. .... fancy ....

1) My **hobbys** are acting and singing. ....

2) We are **puting** make-up on backstage. ....

3) I'm **scareed** I'll forget my lines. ....

4) The show is in **Juligh**. ....

5) I **hurryed** to get dressed. ....

6) The **stadge** is so big. ....

7) The show is a **musicel**. ....

8) Linda has **ritten** a play. ....

Today I scored [ ] out of 8.

Year 2 English — Spring Term

Week 3 — Day 3

Tick the box where a comma should go in each sentence.

Her badge is large ✓ shiny ☐ and gold.

1) The firefighters have a ladder ☐ a hose and ☐ helmets.

2) Ben ☐ Katie ☐ and Aminah are firefighters.

3) We put ☐ out fires ☐ rescue cats ☐ and help people.

4) Is the fire ☐ in the house ☐ the shop ☐ or the bakery?

5) The fire engine is ☐ red ☐ white and ☐ yellow.

6) I work ☐ Monday ☐ Tuesday ☐ and Friday.

7) The helmets ☐ gloves ☐ and ☐ jackets are there.

8) Mum ☐ Dad and ☐ Gran ☐ called the fire service.

Today I scored ☐ out of 8.

Week 3 — Day 4

Read the text, then answer the questions.

The Northern Lights

Asta's mother didn't enjoy winter in northern Norway. She preferred the summer, where the days were long and light. However, Asta had always felt that there was something special about the darkness of the frosty midwinter days. She loved spending her mornings looking up at the stars that still twinkled in the sky. Sometimes, though, Asta would catch a glimpse of colourful lights dancing above her. That really was magic.

1) Write 'true' or 'false' for each sentence.

Asta's mother loves winter in Norway. ....

The summer days are long in Norway. ....

2) Find and copy a word from the text that means '**chilly**'.

....

3) What does Asta like to do on winter mornings?

....

4) How does Asta feel when she sees the '**colourful lights**'?

scared ☐   amazed ☐   bored ☐

Today I scored ☐ out of 5.

Week 3 — Day 5

Read the text, then answer the questions.

Loch Ness Monster Sighted!

Last Tuesday, a local farmer called Alan rang up the 'Loch Ness Monster Club' to report a sighting. Alan said that he was tending to his sheep by the loch when he saw a **lardge** head rise up out of the water. The creature then posed for a photo before **diveing** back under the surface. The 'Loch Ness Monster Club' has urged other locals and tourists to contact them if they see the monster.

1. Give the correct spelling of the words in bold.

   lardge .... **diveing** ....

2. What was Alan doing when he saw the Loch Ness monster?

   ....

3. What does the 'Loch Ness Monster Club' say you should do if you see the monster?

   take a photo ☐   let them know ☐

4. Which of these sentences uses commas correctly?

   The monster survives on fish, plants and, cake. ☐

   The monster survives on fish, plants and cake. ☐

Today I scored ☐ out of 5.

Week 4 — Day 1

Read each sentence. Circle 'yes' or 'no' to show whether the word in bold is spelt correctly.

I **called** him over.   ⓨes   no

1. Connor cleaned his horse's **stall**.   yes   no

2. I **allways** feed the horses in the morning.   yes   no

3. The horse chased after the **borll**.   yes   no

4. Tim didn't want to **fall** off his horse.   yes   no

5. The friendly pony is very **smal**.   yes   no

6. Daisy runs **almost** as fast as Clover.   yes   no

7. My horse ate **all** the hay.   yes   no

8. Keith **tallks** to his pony.   yes   no

9. I'm not **tall** enough to ride the horse.   yes   no

Today I scored ☐ out of 9.

Week 4 — Day 2

Write one of these punctuation marks at the end of each sentence to finish them correctly.

! ?

What are we building…?…

1. How heavy that brick is……..
2. Where is the hammer……..
3. When should we take a tea break……..
4. What a nice job we've done……..
5. Watch out for that digger……..
6. How long will it take to build the wall……..
7. Turn the truck off now……..
8. Why did you make that……..
9. How tired I am……..
10. The house will look great……..

Today I scored ☐ out of 10.

Week 4 — Day 3

Add either 'o' or 'u' to the words in bold to complete the sentences.

M...o...ther is very cross.

1) Mona's dads made us pancakes on **M.......nday**.

2) We took **an.......ther** family photograph.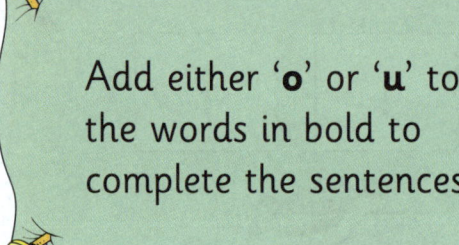

3) My aunt is wearing **gl.......ves**.

4) My little **br.......ther** is so annoying.

5) Grandma baked some iced **b.......ns**.

6) I bought my grandad a **m.......g** for his birthday.

7) Vinny **l.......ves** playing football with his cousin.

8) We like visiting our aunt and **.......ncle**.

9) My sister is **c.......vered** in mud again.

Today I scored [ ] out of 9.

Week 4 — Day 4

Read the poem, then answer the questions.

The Fridge Monster

I don't mind the monster under my bed,
It's the fridge monster that I really dread.
He grumbles and roars all night long,
And sings the most terrible song.
But the thing that I find really rude,
Is that he likes to eat my food.
I wanted something nice to munch,
But the greedy monster ate my lunch!

1) Which monster does the narrator dislike the most?

the monster under the bed ☐   the fridge monster ☐

2) Write down one noise that the fridge monster makes.

....

3) Which word means the same as '**terrible**'?

afraid ☐   awful ☐   delightful ☐

4) What does the narrator find the most annoying about the fridge monster?

....

Today I scored ☐ out of 4.

Week 4 — Day 5

Read the text, then answer the questions.

How To Make A Fruit Salad

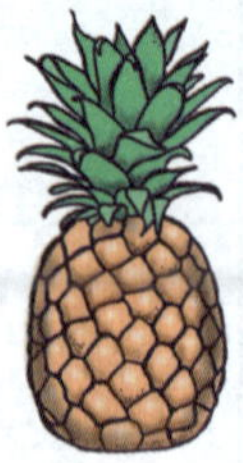

1. Pick your favourite fruit. You should use five or more different types of fruit.
2. Chop up your fruit so that the pieces are about the same size. If using apples, remove the core.
3. Toss **awl** the fruit into a bowl and mix it together. For added sweetness, add a small amount of honey.
4. **Cuver** the bowl and keep your fruit salad in the fridge until you are ready to eat it.

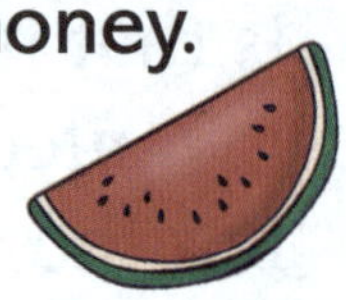

1) Write the correct spelling of the words in bold.

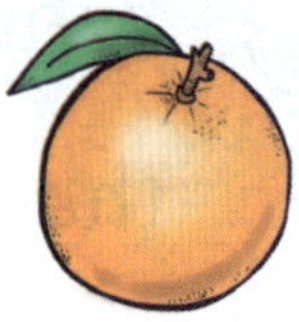

awl ....   cuver ....

2) Circle 'true' or 'false' for this sentence.

You should only use five fruits.   **true / false**

3) According to the text, what can you add to make the fruit salad sweeter?

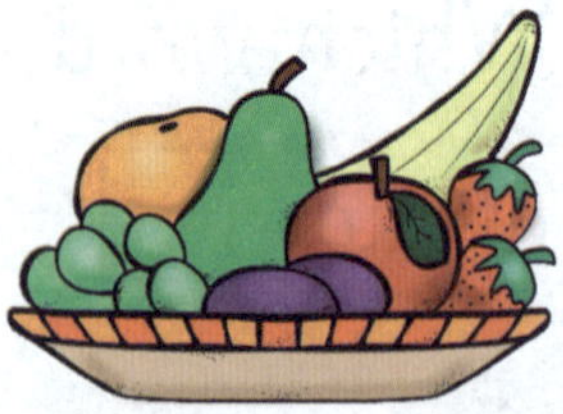

....

4) Write a question mark or an exclamation mark on the line to finish the sentence correctly.

How much fruit do I need........

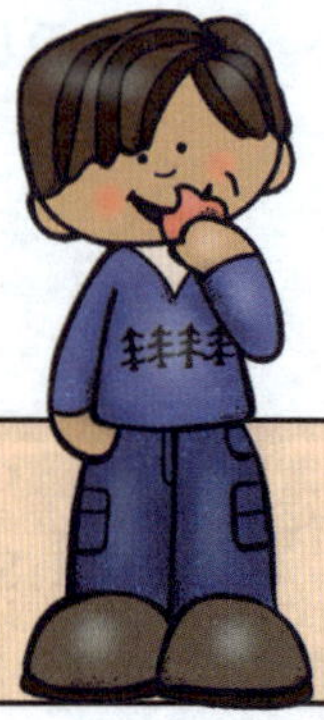

Today I scored ☐ out of 5.

Week 5 — Day 1

Read each sentence. Then circle the letter or letters missing from the word.

We have the **k**__. (ey) ie

1) We saved enough **mon**__ to buy a cottage. ey ie

2) The cottage is **ver**__ old. ie y

3) It is in a quiet **vall**__. y ey

4) There is a small fireplace and a **chimn**__. ie ey

5) I will live there with my **aunt**__. ee ie

6) We could collect **hon**__ from the bees. ee ey

7) We can keep a pet **donk**__ in the field. ey y

8) It is such a **prett**__ place. y ey

Today I scored ☐ out of 8.

Week 5 — Day 2

Add either 'er' or 'ness' to each of the words in bold to turn them into nouns.

I am a **wait**.er......... . er   ness

1. The **work**............... is doing a great job.

2. Athletes have good **fit**............... levels.

3. The nurse is known for her **kind**............... .

4. The **clean**............... comes twice a week.

5. My sister is a **garden**............... .

6. The doctor cured my **ill**............... .

7. The **teach**............... explains things well.

8. I want to be a **paint**............... .

9. The baker's biggest **weak**............... is pastry.

Today I scored ☐ out of 9.

Week 5 — Day 3

Add an apostrophe to each of the words in bold below.

Matt's pencil case is here.

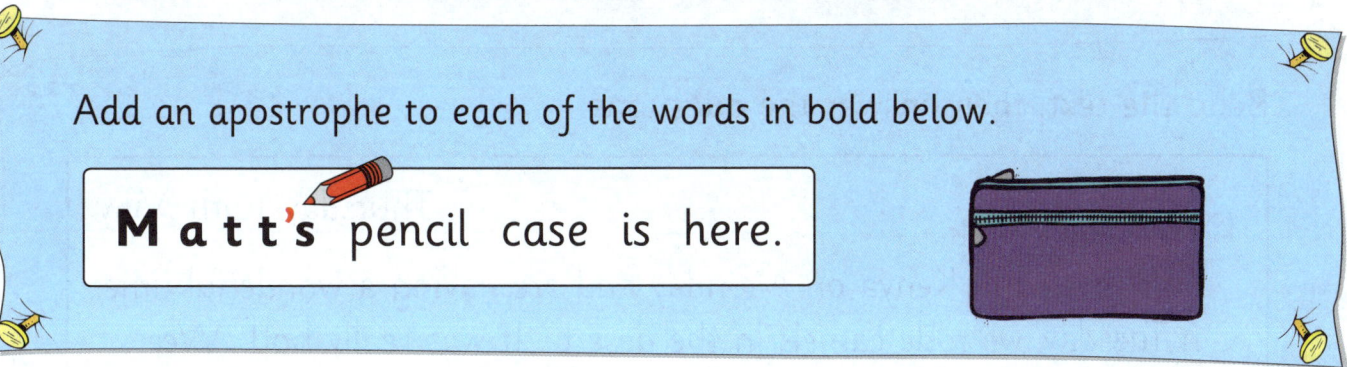

(1) I borrowed **Meeras** ruler.

(2) **Georges** colouring pencils are in a pot.

(3) We used the **teachers** ink pen.

(4) **Noahs** scissors are broken.

(5) Fred stole **Kats** crayons.

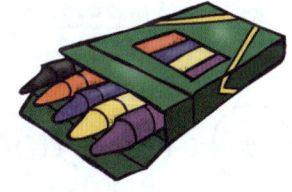

(6) **Avas** glue stick is green.

(7) I found **Dans** pencil sharpener.

(8) **Imogens** highlighters are so bright.

Today I scored [ ] out of 8.

Week 5 — Day 4

Read the text, then answer the questions.

Thursday 10th May

Dear Zadie,
    We arrived in Kenya on Monday and are having a wonderful time. On Tuesday, we rode camels in the desert. It was really hot! We went swimming yesterday and today we are going on safari to see some wild animals. Hopefully we will see some lions and elephants. My sister is a bit scared, but I can't wait! I wish you were here.
From, Henry

1) Write down a word from the text that means 'very good'.

....

2) When did Henry go swimming? Tick one box.

Tuesday ☐   Wednesday ☐   Thursday ☐

3) How does Henry feel about going on safari?

....

4) Tick the two sentences below that are true.

Henry rode a camel yesterday. ☐

Henry is going on safari today. ☐

Zadie is not on holiday in Kenya. ☐

Today I scored ☐ out of 5.

Week 5 — Day 5

Read the text, then answer the questions.

Sloths

Sloths live in the rainforests of Central and South America. They are known for being cute and for being very slow. This means that sloths don't usually travel very far. However, they are good swimmers and can move more quickly when swimming than when they're on the ground or in trees. A sloth's diet is mainly made up of leaves, but they sometimes munch on insects too.

1) What type of word is '**swimmers**'? Tick one box.

adjective ☐   noun ☐   verb ☐

2) Write 'true' or 'false' for each sentence.

Sloths are quicker on ground than in water. ....

Sloths don't normally travel very far. ....

3) Write down two things sloths eat.

.... and ....

4) Tick the phrase that uses an apostrophe for possession.

sloths don't ☐   **A sloth's diet** ☐

Today I scored ☐ out of 6.

Week 6 — Day 1

Add either 'o' or 'a' to the words in bold to complete the sentences.

He w..**a**..nts to have a bath.

1) He woke up as his room felt too **h**........**t**.

2) The babies slept in their **c**........**ts**.

3) I had orange **squ**........**sh** before bed.

4) I use soap to **w**........**sh** my face.

5) My **w**........**tch** shows it is time for bed.

6) She wore thick **s**........**cks** in bed.

7) My bedtime **w**........**s** later than hers.

8) They always **qu**........**rrel** at bedtime.

Today I scored [ ] out of 8.

Week 6 — Day 2

Use the letters in the boxes to complete the words. Then use the letters marked with pink dots to uncover the final word.

That cake is the s .m. a l l e .s. .t. . | m s t |

1) I think that cake was the | n i .... t | one. | s e c |

2) Her cake is a | l ..... g h t .... | colour than his. | e i r |

3) Your cupcakes are | ..... a s t .... r | than mine. | e i t |

4) That is the | t h ..... c k ..... s ..... | icing. | t i e |

5) Next time, I will make a | ..... i g ..... e ..... | cake. | r b g |

6) | ..... w .... e ..... |

Today I scored ☐ out of 6.

Week 6 — Day 3

Read each sentence. Add an apostrophe in the correct place to the word in bold.

That's my bike.

1) **W e r e** going on a bike ride.

2) **I t s** nice weather for cycling today.

3) **W e l l** stop for lunch on the way.

4) The trip **w o n t** take very long.

5) I **c a n t** pedal as fast as my dad.

6) That **i s n t** the right way to go.

7) **D o n t** forget to wear suncream.

8) **H e s** going to ride down the ramp.

9) **T h e y r e** going along the cycle path.

Today I scored ☐ out of 9.

Week 6 — Day 4

Read the text, then answer the questions.

The Hopeful Singer

Charlie wanted to join the school choir because he thought they sounded like angels. The trouble was, he was scared to sing in front of other people. Whenever he tried, his voice was shaky and quiet.

"Try to focus on the feelings in the song," his sister said.

Charlie put on some music. This time, he followed his sister's advice rather than thinking about who was watching him. Then he began to sing. He sounded just like an angel.

1) What did Charlie think the choir sounded like?

....

2) What problem did Charlie have?

....

....

3) What advice did Charlie's sister give him?

take singing lessons ☐

think about the feelings in the song ☐

4) How do you think Charlie feels at the end of the text?

annoyed ☐   happy ☐   nervous ☐

Today I scored ☐ out of 4.

Week 6 — Day 5

Read the text, then answer the questions.

Join Gymnastics Club!
Come to gymnastics club to get fit and make friends!
<u>Some things you might learn</u>: • handstands • cartwheels • forward rolls
<u>Time</u>: Fridays after school   <u>Place</u>: the school hall
<u>**Whot** to bring</u>: your sports kit, a water bottle and lots of energy!
If you're not sure, come and watch the first lesson.

1) Write the correct spelling of the word in bold.

   Whot ....

2) Write down these details about gymnastics club.

   When it happens: ....

   Where it happens: ....

3) Circle the correct option to complete the sentence below.

   Handstands are **easier / the easiest** than cartwheels.

4) Tick the sentence which uses an apostrophe correctly.

   At gymnastics club, you'll learn new skills. ☐

   At gymnastics club, youl'l learn new skills. ☐

Today I scored ☐ out of 5.

Week 7 — Day 1

Read each sentence, then circle the correct spelling of the word in bold.

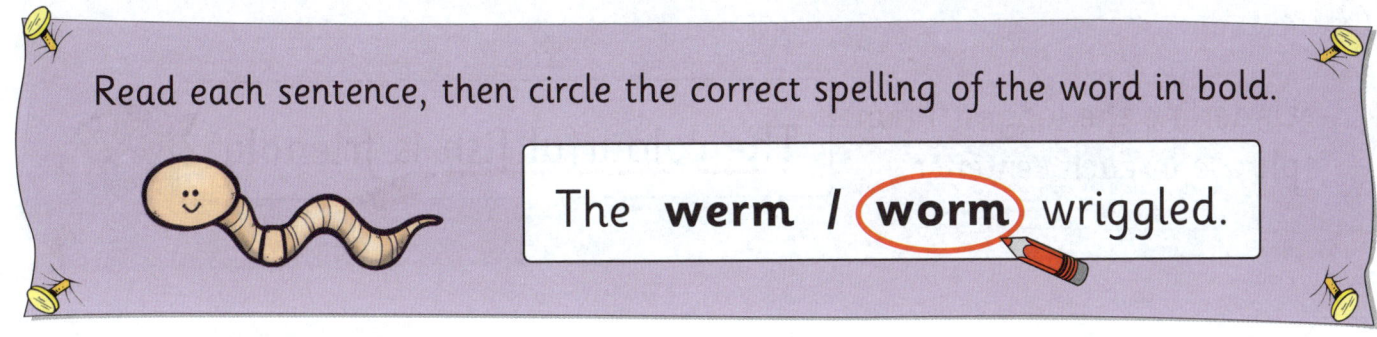

The **werm** / **(worm)** wriggled.

(1) The plant looks **worse** / **werse** than it did yesterday.

(2) My mum **wirks** / **works** as a gardener.

(3) Caring for nature is a **wurthy** / **worthy** cause.

(4) Digging is the **worst** / **wurst** part of gardening.

(5) It is the tallest tree in the **wurld** / **world**.

(6) The flowers **wership** / **worship** the sun.

(7) The flowers are **worth** / **wirth** a lot of money.

(8) The seed label was **wurded** / **worded** oddly.

Today I scored ☐ out of 8.

Week 7 — Day 2

Underline the longest noun phrase in each sentence.

The colourful fish is friendly.

1) The mermaid has a beautiful tail.

2) The blue waves crash onto the beach.

3) A small, orange crab said hello to the fish.

4) A big family of pink fish swam past the seaweed.

5) Swimming is Josh's favourite hobby.

6) The mermaid has long, shiny, golden hair.

7) A graceful, blue dolphin leaps out of the water.

8) The shark grinned and showed its sharp, white teeth.

9) Lottie is singing an amazing song about mermaids.

Today I scored ☐ out of 9.

Week 7 — Day 3

Circle the correct word to complete each sentence.

Ella was feeds (feeding) her dog.

1. Terri was | washing | washed | her muddy dog.

2. They | was | were | barking loudly.

3. Rex was | runs | running | up a hill.

4. Monty and Patch were | eating | eat |.

5. The puppy | were | was | playing.

6. Rob's dog was | being | been | naughty.

7. They were | walks | walking | in the park.

8. Rover was | chews | chewing | a bone.

Today I scored ☐ out of 8.

Week 7 — Day 4

Read the poem, then answer the questions.

Alien Adventure

As Jane was looking at the stars,
She gave a big, sad sigh.
"I wish that I could fly up there,
to see the world and sky."
So imagine Jane's excitement,
When an alien came to stay!
He showed her how to fly his ship,
and they explored space every day.

1) What does Jane do when she looks at the stars?

sings ☐   sighs ☐   smiles ☐

2) Write down one thing that Jane wishes for.

....

3) Why do you think Jane is excited when the alien comes to stay?

....

4) Which word means the same as '**explored**'?

walked ☐   climbed ☐   travelled around ☐

Today I scored ☐ out of 4.

Week 7 — Day 5

Read the text, then answer the questions.

Cowboy School

It was Kieran's first day at school. He was nervous. What if he was the **wurst** cowboy? A small girl with a huge grin greeted him. "Howdy!" she said, "I'm Connie. I can't wait to show you around!" Kieran smiled. He wasn't as nervous now that he had a friend. The day was full of riding lessons, line dancing and other classes. Kieran loved every minute. He even enjoyed doing his **homewerk**!

1) Give the correct spelling of the words in bold.

wurst ....   **homewerk** ....

2) Write 'true' or 'false' for each sentence.

Kieran wasn't nervous at first. ....

Kieran enjoyed his first day. ....

3) Write down the noun phrase that describes Connie.

....

4) Which of these sentences makes sense? Tick one box.

Kieran and Connie were riding horses. ☐

Kieran and Connie were ride horses. ☐

Today I scored ☐ out of 6.

Week 8 — Day 1

Read each sentence. Circle 'yes' or 'no' to show whether the word in bold is spelt correctly.

He stole the **award**.   (yes)   no

1. **Warning** — there's a criminal on the loose.   yes   no

2. He has a **wart** on his nose.   yes   no

3. Maya **swore** she would catch him.   yes   no

4. She took her uniform out of the **wordrobe**.   yes   no

5. There is a **rewored** for information.   yes   no

6. Maya **warked** into the police station.   yes   no

7. He was seen running **towards** the airport.   yes   no

8. It was **warm** in the back of the police car.   yes   no

Today I scored ☐ out of 8.

Week 8 — Day 2

Circle the word in the correct tense to complete each sentence.

Earlier, she wrote a song and **(sang)** / **sings** it.

1) Every week, Lily sings and Lee **plays** / **played** guitar.

2) We **won** / **win** tickets to the concert yesterday.

3) We **practise** / **practised** daily and perform on Fridays.

4) I **listen** / **listened** to rock music while I do homework.

5) I **went** / **go** home after the concert finished.

6) I **made** / **make** music posters last week.

7) Kai listened to the song and **dances** / **danced**.

8) The singer **has** / **had** brown hair and wears boots.

9) Mo went out and **buys** / **bought** our album.

10) We **released** / **release** a new song earlier.

Today I scored ☐ out of 10.

Week 8 — Day 3

Read each sentence. Write 'S' next to the statements, 'E' next to the exclamations, 'Q' next to the questions and 'C' next to the commands.

I really like science. ....S....

1) Our science teacher is the best. ....

2) Don't touch that, Bianca. ....

3) What an exciting experiment! ....

4) Should this change colour? ....

5) Wear your safety goggles. ....

6) We are learning about space. ....

7) How do magnets work? ....

8) I am going to the lab. ....

9) Mix these two things together. ....

10) How interesting these results are! ....

Today I scored [ ] out of 10.

Year 2 English — Spring Term   © CGP — Not to be photocopied

Week 8 — Day 4

Read the text, then answer the questions.

Volcanic Eruptions

- A volcano is a hole in the surface of the earth that is full of magma (hot, melted rock).
- When the magma builds up, the volcano erupts, launching ash and lava into the sky. Lava is the name for magma once it has left the volcano.
- After an eruption, the lava cools and turns back into solid rock.
- Some mountains in the UK used to be active volcanoes. They are now extinct, which means they won't erupt again.

1) Which word means the same as 'launching'?

taking ☐   throwing ☐   making ☐

2) Write down one thing that comes out of a volcano.

....

3) What happens to lava after an eruption?

....

4) Put a tick next to the sentences that are true. Tick two.

Lava is found inside volcanoes. ☐

There used to be active volcanoes in the UK. ☐

Extinct volcanoes don't erupt. ☐

Today I scored ☐ out of 5.

Week 8 — Day 5

Read the text, then answer the questions.

The Clock Maker

The clock maker made all sorts of clocks. He made big ones, small ones and cuckoo clocks. One day, I went to his shop only to find that he wasn't there. As I waited, I fiddled with a strange clock on the counter. Suddenly, the room began to spin. I shouted, but the spinning stopped almost as quickly as it had begun. I ran to the window and saw that there was a horse where my bike had been. Everyone was also wearing old-fashioned clothes. How odd it was!

1 Write down one type of clock made by the clock maker.

....

2 Write the numbers 1 to 3 in the boxes below to show the order of events in the text.

The narrator shouted. ☐

The room started spinning. ☐

The narrator ran to the window. ☐

3 What type of sentence is '**How odd it was!**'?

exclamation ☐   command ☐   statement ☐

4 What do you think has happened to the narrator?

....

Today I scored ☐ out of 6.

Week 9 — Day 1

Read each sentence, then circle the correct spelling of the word in bold.

It was an **unushual** / **unusual** TV show.

1) There was an **explozion** / **explosion** in the TV show.

2) Joe **usually** / **uzually** watches TV on Saturday.

3) I watch TV for **pleasure** / **pleasjure**.

4) The show is about **Azia** / **Asia**.

5) Delia wears glasses to improve her **vision** / **vizzion**.

6) Obasi watches TV in his **leishure** / **leisure** time.

7) We watch **televijion** / **television** after school.

8) This **verzion** / **version** of the show is better.

Today I scored ☐ out of 8.

Week 9 — Day 2

Add a comma in the right place in each sentence.

Mary, Hugh and Liam can fly.

1. Ila practises flying on Monday Friday and Sunday.

2. She can dance fly and twirl in the air.

3. Karim Jay and Laura have magical powers.

4. Terry makes potions spells and charms.

5. Pick one two or three petals.

6. Mix in a leaf some honey and a flower.

7. Add a daisy a feather and some stardust.

Today I scored ☐ out of 7.

Week 9 — Day 3

Read each pair of sentences. Tick the sentence that uses an adverb correctly.

The frog croaked loudily. ☐
The frog croaked loudly. ✓

1. Sal held tightly to the branch. ☐
   Sal held tightely to the branch. ☐

2. The parrot flew speedily over the rainforest. ☐
   The parrot flew speedyly over the rainforest. ☐

3. Chad swung playful through the trees. ☐
   Chad swung playfully through the trees. ☐

4. Bill hopped quickly across the forest floor. ☐
   Bill hopped quickily across the forest floor. ☐

5. The gorillas carefully searched for food. ☐
   The gorillas carefuly searched for food. ☐

6. The crocodile swam swift through the cool water. ☐
   The crocodile swam swiftly through the cool water. ☐

Today I scored ☐ out of 6.

Week 9 — Day 4

Read the text, then answer the questions.

Aztec Food Fact File

The Aztecs lived hundreds of years ago in the place we now call Mexico. They were skilled at hunting and farming, and ate lots of foods that we still eat today. The Aztecs didn't eat much meat, but they ate lots of fruit, corn and beans. They also made a chocolate drink from cacao beans. These beans were treasured by the Aztecs, and they even used them as a form of money!

1) Tick the sentence below that is true.

The Aztecs are one hundred years old. ☐

The Aztecs ate some of the same foods we do. ☐

2) Write down one thing that the Aztecs were good at.

....

3) Which of these foods did the Aztecs eat a lot of?

meat ☐   corn ☐   potatoes ☐

4) Write down one way the Aztecs used cacao beans.

....

Today I scored ☐ out of 4.

Week 9 — Day 5

Read the text, then answer the questions.

The Roar

The ground shook as a loud roar echoed through the tall trees.
"That's **unuzual**," said Dave, looking around in confusion. "Normally, the only sounds we hear in these woods are birds singing **sweetlly** and the leaves rustling gently in the breeze."

Karen frowned. Suddenly, there was another roar — it was even louder than before. Dave and Karen looked at each other in fear as a huge animal came crashing through the trees. It was a dinosaur!

1) Write the correct spellings of the words in bold.

unuzual .... **sweetlly** ....

2) Which word means the same as '**gently**'?

loudly ☐   quickly ☐   wildly ☐   softly ☐

3) Tick the sentence that uses commas correctly.

The trees, leaves and, ground shook. ☐

The trees, leaves and ground shook. ☐

4) What is making the roaring sound?

....

Today I scored ☐ out of 5.

Week 10 — Day 1

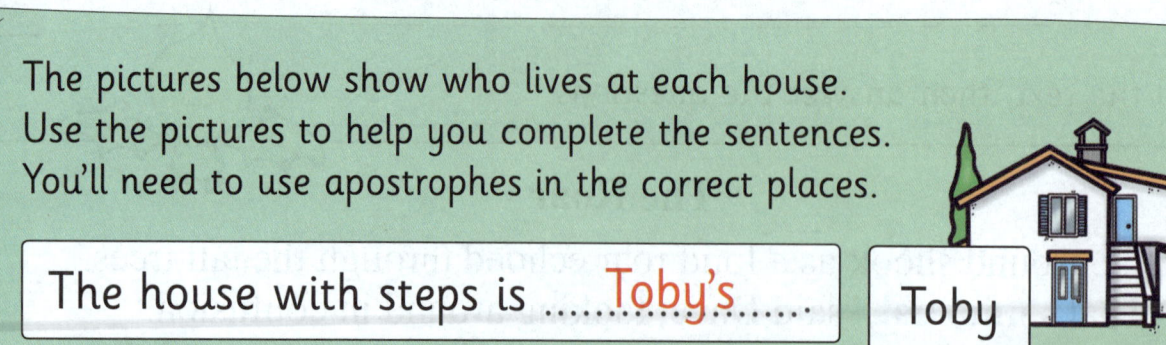

The pictures below show who lives at each house. Use the pictures to help you complete the sentences. You'll need to use apostrophes in the correct places.

The house with steps is ......Toby's...... Toby

1) The house with two chimneys is ....

2) .... house has grass at the front.

3) The house with the gate is ....

4) .... house only has one floor.

5) .... house has a red door.

Today I scored [ ] out of 5.

Week 10 — Day 2

Add either '**ment**' or '**ness**' to the words in bold to complete the sentences.

The party games caused a lot of **excite**.ment........

1) Ollie has a **fond**.............. for birthday parties.

2) Mel got a lot of **enjoy**.............. out of her new toy.

3) They came to an **agree**.............. about which cake to have.

4) Alice cried with **sad**.............. when it was time to leave.

5) James asked for **forgive**.............. after arriving late.

6) The children cheered with **happi**..............

7) A clown provided **entertain**..............

8) After a bit of **encourage**.............., Lizo joined the game.

Today I scored ☐ out of 8.

Week 10 — Day 3

Write a noun phrase to describe each picture.  a yellow and white cake

1.

2.

3.

4.

5.

Today I scored ☐ out of 5.

Week 10 — Day 4

Read the text, then answer the questions.

The Vikings

The Vikings were a group of people from Norway, Sweden and Denmark. They were expert sailors who travelled across the world in wooden boats called longboats. They sailed to many countries, including France, Iceland and the UK. They even got as far as Canada. Today, we would use modern technology to help us sail such long distances without getting lost, but the Vikings knew how to use the position of the Sun and stars to find their way across the vast oceans.

1) Give one country that the Vikings came from.

....

2) Which word in the text means the same as '**huge**'?

expert ☐   modern ☐   vast ☐   wooden ☐

3) Write 'true' or 'false' for each sentence.

The Vikings never reached Canada. ....

Viking boats were made of metal. ....

4) Give two things the Vikings used to make sure they were going in the right direction when they were sailing.

.... and ....

Today I scored ☐ out of 6.

Week 10 — Day 5

Read the poem, then answer the questions.

Mila's Surprises

Mila's school bag is large and blue,
And every day she puts in something new.
When the school day is over and lessons complete,
Everyone gathers to see today's treat.
The children around her have mouths open wide,
As they look to find out what she's got inside.
It might be a ball or an old cricket bat,
Or perhaps her mum's shoes or her grandfather's hat!

1) Tick the sentence below that is true.

People gather around Mila before school starts. ☐

Mila brings a different item each day. ☐

2) Give one word to describe how the children feel when Mila shows them what's in her bag.

....

3) Write a noun phrase to describe this picture.

....

4) Circle the correct suffix for the word in bold.

The children gasped in **amaze** ment / ness .

Today I scored ☐ out of 4.

Week 11 — Day 1

Read each pair of sentences. Then tick the sentence which makes sense.

They were having a water fight. ✓
They were have a water fight. ☐

1. Ali were firing water at Anne. ☐
   Ali was firing water at Anne. ☐

2. Viraj and Ruth was laughing. ☐
   Viraj and Ruth were laughing. ☐

3. Celia was throwing water balloons at us. ☐
   Celia were throwing water balloons at us. ☐

4. They were hiding from the water fight. ☐
   They were hides from the water fight. ☐

5. We were runned away from Jed. ☐
   We were running away from Jed. ☐

6. Christina was planned her next attack. ☐
   Christina was planning her next attack. ☐

7. Neil was dripping with cold water. ☐
   Neil was dripped with cold water. ☐

Today I scored ☐ out of 7.

Week 11 — Day 2

Read each sentence, then circle the correct spelling of the word in bold.

There are six rooms in **toetal** / **total**.

1) Mum is cleaning the rug in the **haul** / **hall**.

2) There is a **monkey** / **monkie** in the kitchen.

3) Dad put the biscuits in the **uven** / **oven**.

4) My whole family **squashed** / **squoshed** onto the sofa.

5) Dani's maths homework was about **division** / **divisheon**.

6) The monkey hid in the **wordrobe** / **wardrobe**.

7) His bedroom is his favourite place in the **world** / **werld**.

8) The new chair was a big **improvement** / **improvment**.

Today I scored ☐ out of 8.

Week 11 — Day 3

Write one of these suffixes (word endings) in each gap to turn the words in bold into adjectives.

ful   less

The **help** ful......... cat showed Bako the way.

1) The grey kitten is very **play**...............

2) Her **care**............... cat fell off the wall again.

3) The **fear**............... kitten jumped without a second thought.

4) My cat has **colour**............... orange and brown stripes.

5) My greedy cat ate **count**............... treats.

6) The sleeping cat looks very **peace**...............

7) Tabitha made a **dread**............... growling sound.

8) My cat wouldn't eat the **taste**............... food.

9) I cried when the cat scratched me — it was **pain**...............

Today I scored ☐ out of 9.

Week 11 — Day 4

Read the text, then answer the questions.

Agent Ruby

Ruby sat on the plane. She had been training to be a secret agent her whole life. She had learned five languages, could easily avoid being seen and was great at locating hidden information. When the day came for her first real mission, she was nervous. She had prepared so much and wanted it to be a success. The pilot announced they had arrived. Ruby put on her parachute and opened the door.

1) Which of these did Ruby learn to do during her training?

speak different languages ☐   fly a plane ☐

2) Find and copy a word that means 'finding'.

....

3) Why do you think Ruby feels nervous?

It's her first real mission. ☐   She is unprepared. ☐

4) What do you think will happen next in the story?

....

....

Today I scored ☐ out of 4.

Week 11 — Day 5

Read the text, then answer the questions.

Wimbledon

- Wimbledon is a tennis competition that happens every summer in London. Only skilled and **successfull** players can take part.
- The event first took place over 140 years ago, in 1877.
- It has some strange traditions. For example, the players must wear white clothes otherwise they won't be allowed to play.
- The spectators eat a huge **quontity** of strawberries and cream.

1 Give the correct spelling of the words in bold.

successfull ....   **quontity** ....

2 What happens if a player doesn't wear white clothes?

....

3 Tick the sentence that uses the past tense with 'ing'.

He was playing in the final match. ☐

He playing in the final match yesterday. ☐

4 Write 'true' or 'false' for each sentence.

Wimbledon takes place in December. ....

Strawberries are popular at Wimbledon. ....

Today I scored ☐ out of 6.

Week 12 — Day 1

Read the sentences and circle the correct spelling of the words in bold. Then draw lines to match each person to their bag.

Tim's case is the **shortist** / **shortest**.

1) Shane's case is in **frunt** / **front** of the blue case.

2) Sabira's bag matches her **gloves** / **gluves**.

3) Raven's case is the **torllest** / **tallest**.

4) Lisa's case is overflowing with **treasure** / **treazure**.

5) Arlo's bag is next to the one with the **donkey** / **donkie**.

Today I scored ☐ out of 10.

Week 12 — Day 2

Circle the correct word to complete each sentence.

We love it | because | (when) | it rains.

1) Take a raincoat | if | that | you go outside.

2) We were playing | when | if | it started to rain.

3) I don't care | if | because | I get wet.

4) I took a jacket | because | that | it was cold.

5) That's the umbrella | when | that | I want.

6) I'll wear the boots | that | because | I like.

7) He got wet | that | when | he jumped in the puddle.

8) This is the storm | if | that | was forecast.

Today I scored ☐ out of 8.

© CGP — Not to be photocopied
Year 2 English — Spring Term

Week 12 — Day 3

Read each sentence, then shorten the words in bold using an apostrophe.

We are going on a scavenger hunt. ...... We're ......

1) **I will** go and look over here. ....

2) I **cannot** see anything. ....

3) **She has** found the first item. ....

4) **They are** searching in the woods. ....

5) Look at what **we have** found. ....

6) **What is** next on the list? ....

7) The other team **are not** going to win. ....

Today I scored ☐ out of 7.

Week 12 — Day 4

Read the text, then answer the questions.

Quick Cats

Cheetahs are the fastest land animal in the world. These fierce creatures can run at speeds of around 70 miles per hour — that's the same speed that a car can go on the motorway. They have long, powerful legs to help them run quickly. While they are running, their sharp claws dig into the ground to prevent them from slipping. Running this fast uses up a lot of energy, so they can only do it for less than a minute at a time.

(1) What does the word 'fierce' suggest about cheetahs?

They are dangerous. ☐ They are furry. ☐

(2) Give two body parts that help cheetahs to run.

.... and ....

(3) What do you think 'prevent' might mean?

allow ☐   help ☐   stop ☐   grip ☐

(4) Why can't cheetahs run for very long?

....

....

Today I scored ☐ out of 5.

Week 12 — Day 5

Read the poem, then answer the questions.

Growing Up

The twins would quarrel all the time,
About which one of them was taller.
Since they could not agree, they **meazured** themselves,
And it turned out that Sam was **smorler**.
So Sam planted himself in the ground like a tree,
And began to grow like no other.
After three long days in the garden soil,
He was ten times the height of his brother.

1) Give the correct spelling of the words in bold.

meazured .... **smorler** ....

2) What do you think the word '**quarrel**' might mean?

talk ☐   argue ☐   laugh ☐   play ☐

3) Write '**could not**' using an apostrophe.

....

4) Give one word to describe how you think Sam felt when he found out that he was shorter than his brother.

....

Today I scored ☐ out of 5.

Answers

Week 1 — Day 1
1. There is an interesting foss**il** here.
2. Do you **kn**ow where the vase is from?
3. My brother prefers the scien**ce** museum.
4. The rub**ies** are in the museum.
5. The statue is hu**ge**.
6. They dug up some old met**al** tools.
7. The old **wr**iting is interesting.
8. There are a lot of peop**le** here.

Week 1 — Day 2
1. <u>maria</u> always wanted to be a ballerina.
2. The best dancer in the class is <u>steve</u>.
3. I do tap dancing every <u>monday</u>.
4. My brother and <u>i</u> love to dance.
5. <u>my</u> tap teacher is a beautiful dancer.
6. Sonya studies dance in <u>russia</u>.
7. I danced with <u>ed</u>.
8. I went to see a dance show in <u>paris</u>.
9. My mum told me the show is on <u>sunday</u>.
10. <u>there</u> is a tiny dancer in the music box.

Week 1 — Day 3
1. fingerprint
2. raincoat
3. sunset
4. eyeball
5. seahorse
6. starfish
7. E.g. buttercup / butterfly

Week 1 — Day 4
1. Salmon spend most of their lives in the ocean.
2. incredible
3. to lay eggs
4. hungry bears

Week 1 — Day 5
1. greedy, little
   (1 mark for each)
2. past tense
3. the café owner
4. Percy ate it.

Week 2 — Day 1
1. Tom **carried** some books.
2. There are two **libraries** in our town.
3. We read the first **page** together.
4. They tried to make the bird **fly** away.
5. Anna's books began to **wobble**.
6. I **placed** the book back on the shelf.
7. Yasmin returned the **funny** book.
8. She is **smiling** about the story.
9. My book is about a **gnome**.

Week 2 — Day 2
1. My mum, dad **and** sister all came with me.
2. Pick either an ice cream **or** a lolly.
3. It rained a lot **but** we still had fun.
4. We went by car **and** then by plane.
5. That suitcase is either mine **or** Juan's.
6. We can go swimming **or** hiking, but not both.
7. We got lost **but** luckily we had a map.

Week 2 — Day 3
1. Eva polished her flute to make it **shinier**.
2. Shhh, this part of the music is **quieter**.
3. The trumpets made the **loudest** sound.
4. Umar found this part the **easiest** to play.
5. Lea hit the drum **harder** to make more noise.
6. Hurry, this part should be the **fastest**.

Week 2 — Day 4
1. on streets
2. bats and mice
   (1 mark for each)
3. E.g. The animals they eat come out at night.
4. twit twoo

Week 2 — Day 5
1. Kim's treehouse is **higher** than her actual house.
2. a tent / some leaves
3. and
4. Kim thinks that she won't be found.

Week 3 — Day 1

	¹k	n	i	²f	e	
				r		³b
			⁴c		i		a
			e		e		g
	⁵f	r	i	d	g	e
			e				l
			a				s
⁶k	e	t	t	l	e	

Week 3 — Day 2
1. hobbies
2. putting
3. scared
4. July
5. hurried
6. stage
7. musical
8. written

Week 3 — Day 3
1. The firefighters have a ladder, a hose and helmets.
2. Ben, Katie and Aminah are firefighters.
3. We put out fires, rescue cats and help people.
4. Is the fire in the house, the shop or the bakery?
5. The fire engine is red, white and yellow.
6. I work Monday, Tuesday and Friday.
7. The helmets, gloves and jackets are there.
8. Mum, Dad and Gran called the fire service.

Week 3 — Day 4
1. Asta's mother loves winter in Norway. — false
   The summer days are long in Norway. — true
   (1 mark for each)
2. frosty
3. look up at the stars
4. amazed

Week 3 — Day 5
1. large, diving
   (1 mark for each)
2. tending to his sheep
3. let them know
4. The monster survives on fish, plants and cake.

Week 4 — Day 1
1. yes
2. no
3. no
4. yes
5. no
6. yes
7. yes
8. no
9. yes

Week 4 — Day 2
1. How heavy that brick is!
2. Where is the hammer?
3. When should we take a tea break?
4. What a nice job we've done!
5. Watch out for that digger!
6. How long will it take to build the wall?
7. Turn the truck off now!
8. Why did you make that?
9. How tired I am!
10. The house will look great!

Week 4 — Day 3
1. Mona's dads made us pancakes on M**o**nday.
2. We took an**o**ther family photograph.
3. My aunt is wearing gl**o**ves.
4. My little br**o**ther is so annoying.
5. Grandma baked some iced b**u**ns.
6. I bought my grandad a m**u**g for his birthday.
7. Vinny l**o**ves playing football with his cousin.
8. We like visiting our aunt and **u**ncle.
9. My sister is c**o**vered in mud again.

Week 4 — Day 4
1. the fridge monster
2. he grumbles / he roars / he sings (the most terrible song)
3. awful
4. He eats the narrator's food.

Week 4 — Day 5
1. all, cover
   (1 mark for each)
2. false
3. honey
4. How much fruit do I need?

Week 5 — Day 1
1. We saved enough mon**ey** to buy a cottage.
2. The cottage is ver**y** old.
3. It is in a quiet vall**ey**.
4. There is a small fireplace and a chimn**ey**.
5. I will live there with my aunt**ie**.
6. We could collect hon**ey** from the bees.
7. We can keep a pet donk**ey** in the field.
8. It is such a prett**y** place.

Week 5 — Day 2
1. The work**er** is doing a great job.
2. Athletes have good fit**ness** levels.
3. The nurse is known for her kind**ness**.
4. The clean**er** comes twice a week.
5. My sister is a garden**er**.
6. The doctor cured my ill**ness**.
7. The teach**er** explains things well.
8. I want to be a paint**er**.
9. The baker's biggest weak**ness** is pastry.

Week 5 — Day 3
1. I borrowed Meera's ruler.
2. George's colouring pencils are in a pot.
3. We used the teacher's ink pen.
4. Noah's scissors are broken.
5. Fred stole Kat's crayons.
6. Ava's glue stick is green.
7. I found Dan's pencil sharpener.
8. Imogen's highlighters are so bright.

Week 5 — Day 4
1. wonderful
2. Wednesday
3. He is excited.
4. Henry is going on safari today. Zadie is not on holiday in Kenya.
   (1 mark for each)

Week 5 — Day 5
1. noun
2. Sloths are quicker on ground than in water. — false
   Sloths don't normally travel very far. — true
   (1 mark for each)
3. **leaves** and **insects**
   (1 mark for each)
4. A sloth's diet

Week 6 — Day 1
1. He woke up as his room felt too h**o**t.
2. The babies slept in their c**o**ts.
3. I had orange squ**a**sh before bed.
4. I use soap to w**a**sh my face.
5. My w**a**tch shows it is time for bed.
6. She wore thick s**o**cks in bed.
7. My bedtime w**a**s later than hers.
8. They always qu**a**rrel at bedtime.

Week 6 — Day 2
1. I think that cake was the ni**cest** one.
2. Her cake is a l**ighter** colour than his.
3. Your cupcakes are t**astier** than mine.
4. That is the th**ickest** icing.
5. Next time, I will make a **bigger** cake.
6. **sweeter**

Week 6 — Day 3
1. We're going on a bike ride
2. It's nice weather for cycling today.
3. We'll stop for lunch on the way.
4. The trip won't take very long.
5. I can't pedal as fast as my dad.
6. That isn't the right way to go.
7. Don't forget to wear suncream.
8. He's going to ride down the ramp.
9. They're going along the cycle path.

Week 6 — Day 4
1. angels
2. He was scared to sing in front of other people. / His singing voice was shaky and quiet.
3. think about the feelings in the song
4. happy

Week 6 — Day 5
1. What
2. When it happens: **Fridays after school**
   Where it happens: **the school hall**
   (1 mark for each)
3. Handstands are **easier** than cartwheels.
4. At gymnastics club, you'll learn new skills.

Week 7 — Day 1
1. The plant looks **worse** than it did yesterday.
2. My mum **works** as a gardener.
3. Caring for nature is a **worthy** cause.
4. Digging is the **worst** part of gardening.
5. It is the tallest tree in the **world**.
6. The flowers **worship** the sun.
7. The flowers are **worth** a lot of money.
8. The seed label was **worded** oddly.

Answers

Week 7 — Day 2

1. The mermaid has <u>a beautiful tail</u>.
2. <u>The blue waves</u> crash onto the beach.
3. <u>A small, orange crab</u> said hello to the fish.
4. <u>A big family of pink fish</u> swam past the seaweed.
5. Swimming is <u>Josh's favourite hobby</u>.
6. The mermaid has <u>long, shiny, golden hair</u>.
7. <u>A graceful, blue dolphin</u> leaps out of the water.
8. The shark grinned and showed <u>its sharp, white teeth</u>.
9. Lottie is singing <u>an amazing song about mermaids</u>.

Week 7 — Day 3

1. Terri was **washing** her muddy dog.
2. They **were** barking loudly.
3. Rex was **running** up a hill.
4. Monty and Patch were **eating**.
5. The puppy **was** playing.
6. Rob's dog was **being** naughty.
7. They were **walking** in the park.
8. Rover was **chewing** a bone.

Week 7 — Day 4

1. sighs
2. to fly in space / to see the world / to see the sky
3. E.g. The alien can take her to space.
4. travelled around

Week 7 — Day 5

1. worst, homework (1 mark for each)
2. Kieran wasn't nervous at first. — false
   Kieran enjoyed his first day. — true
   (1 mark for each)
3. A small girl with a huge grin
4. Kieran and Connie were riding horses.

Week 8 — Day 1

1. yes
2. yes
3. yes
4. no
5. no
6. no
7. yes
8. yes

Week 8 — Day 2

1. Every week, Lily sings and Lee **plays** guitar.
2. We **won** tickets to the concert yesterday.
3. We **practise** daily and perform on Fridays.
4. I **listen** to rock music while I do homework.
5. I **went** home after the concert finished.
6. I **made** music posters last week.
7. Kai listened to the song and **danced**.
8. The singer **has** brown hair and wears boots.
9. Mo went out and **bought** our album.
10. We **released** a new song earlier.

Week 8 — Day 3

1. S
2. C
3. E
4. Q
5. C
6. S
7. Q
8. S
9. C
10. E

Week 8 — Day 4

1. throwing
2. ash / lava
3. It cools. / It turns back into rock.
4. There used to be active volcanoes in the UK.
   Extinct volcanoes don't erupt.
   (1 mark for each)

Week 8 — Day 5

1. big clocks / small clocks / cuckoo clocks
2. The narrator shouted. — 2
   The room started spinning. — 1
   The narrator ran to the window. — 3
   (1 mark for each)
3. exclamation
4. E.g. They have gone back in time.

Week 9 — Day 1

1. There was an **explosion** in the TV show.
2. Joe **usually** watches TV on Saturday.
3. I watch TV for **pleasure**.
4. The show is about **Asia**.
5. Delia wears glasses to improve her **vision**.
6. Obasi watches TV in his **leisure** time.
7. We watch **television** after school.
8. This **version** of the show is better.

Week 9 — Day 2

1. Ila practises flying on Monday, Friday and Sunday.
2. She can dance, fly and twirl in the air.
3. Karim, Jay and Laura have magical powers.
4. Terry makes potions, spells and charms.
5. Pick one, two or three petals.
6. Mix in a leaf, some honey and a flower.
7. Add a daisy, a feather and some stardust.

Week 9 — Day 3

1. Sal held **tightly** to the branch.
2. The parrot flew **speedily** over the rainforest.
3. Chad swung **playfully** through the trees.
4. Bill hopped **quickly** across the forest floor.
5. The gorillas **carefully** searched for food.
6. The crocodile swam **swiftly** through the cool water.

Week 9 — Day 4

1. The Aztecs ate some of the same foods we do.
2. hunting / farming
3. corn
4. to make a chocolate drink / as a form of money

Week 9 — Day 5

1. unusual, sweetly (1 mark for each)
2. softly
3. The trees, leaves and ground shook.
4. a dinosaur

Week 10 — Day 1

1. The house with two chimneys is **Jo's**.
2. **Nick's** house has grass at the front.
3. The house with the gate is **Sara's**.
4. **Raj's** house only has one floor.
5. **Amy's** house has a red door.

Week 10 — Day 2
1. Ollie has a fond**ness** for birthday parties.
2. Mel got a lot of enjoy**ment** out of her new toy.
3. They came to an agree**ment** about which cake to have.
4. Alice cried with sad**ness** when it was time to leave.
5. James asked for forgive**ness** after arriving late.
6. The children cheered with happi**ness**.
7. A clown provided entertain**ment**.
8. After a bit of encourage**ment**, Lizo joined the game.

Week 10 — Day 3
1. E.g. a strawberry ice cream cone
2. E.g. the spotty teacup
3. E.g. a tasty sandwich
4. E.g. the jar of orange juice
5. E.g. a plate of cookies

Week 10 — Day 4
1. Norway / Sweden / Denmark
2. vast
3. The Vikings never reached Canada. — false
   Viking boats were made of metal. — false
   (1 mark for each)
4. **the Sun** and **the stars**
   (1 mark for each)

Week 10 — Day 5
1. Mila brings a different item each day.
2. E.g. excited
3. E.g. the stripy beach ball
4. The children gasped in amaze**ment**.

Week 11 — Day 1
1. Ali **was** firing water at Anne.
2. Viraj and Ruth **were** laughing.
3. Celia **was** throwing water balloons at us.
4. They were **hiding** from the water fight.
5. We were **running** away from Jed.
6. Christina was **planning** her next attack.
7. Neil was **dripping** with cold water.

Week 11 — Day 2
1. Mum is cleaning the rug in the **hall**.
2. There is a **monkey** in the kitchen.
3. Dad put the biscuits in the **oven**.
4. My whole family **squashed** onto the sofa.
5. Dani's maths homework was about **division**.
6. The monkey hid in the **wardrobe**.
7. His bedroom is his favourite place in the **world**.
8. The new chair was a big **improvement**.

Week 11 — Day 3
1. The grey kitten is very play**ful**.
2. Her care**less** cat fell off the wall again.
3. The fear**less** kitten jumped without a second thought.
4. My cat has colour**ful** orange and brown stripes.
5. My greedy cat ate count**less** treats.
6. The sleeping cat looks very peace**ful**.
7. Tabitha made a dread**ful** growling sound.
8. My cat wouldn't eat the taste**less** food.
9. I cried when the cat scratched me — it was pain**ful**.

Week 11 — Day 4
1. speak different languages
2. locating
3. It's her first real mission.
4. E.g. She will jump out of the plane.

Week 11 — Day 5
1. successful, quantity
   (1 mark for each)
2. They won't be allowed to play.
3. He was playing in the final match.
4. Wimbledon takes place in December. — false
   Strawberries are popular at Wimbledon. — true
   (1 mark for each)

Week 12 — Day 1
1. Shane's case is in **front** of the blue case.
2. Sabira's bag matches her **gloves**.
3. Raven's case is the **tallest**.
4. Lisa's case is overflowing with **treasure**.
5. Arlo's bag is next to the one with the **donkey**.

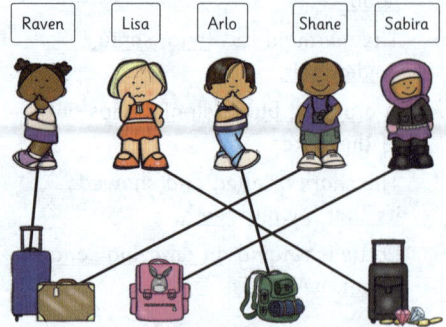

Week 12 — Day 2
1. Take a raincoat **if** you go outside.
2. We were playing **when** it started to rain.
3. I don't care **if** I get wet.
4. I took a jacket **because** it was cold.
5. That's the umbrella **that** I want.
6. I'll wear the boots **that** I like.
7. He got wet **when** he jumped in the puddle.
8. This is the storm **that** was forecast.

Week 12 — Day 3
1. I'll
2. can't
3. She's
4. They're
5. we've
6. What's
7. aren't

Week 12 — Day 4
1. They are dangerous.
2. **legs** and **claws**
   (1 mark for each)
3. stop
4. It uses up a lot of energy (so they get tired quickly).

Week 12 — Day 5
1. measured, smaller
   (1 mark for each)
2. argue
3. couldn't
4. E.g. annoyed

Answers